Richmond

COMPASS

STARTER

Reading LOG

Suzanne Harris
Robert Hill
Esther Mizrachi

Featured Authors
Kelly Bingham
Kenn Nesbitt
Deirdre Sullivan
Debbie Thomas

Richmond

58 St Aldates
Oxford
OX1 1ST
United Kingdom

First Edition: 2019
ISBN: 978-607-06-1575-7

Compass Reading Log Starter Level

Av. Río Mixcoac No. 274, Col. Acacias,
Del. Benito Juárez, C.P. 03240, Ciudad de México

Publisher: Justine Piekarowicz
Project Manager: Amanda Guppy
Editor: Kimberly MacCurdy
Design: Orlando Llanas, Erika Martínez
Layout: Aphik S.A. de C.V.
Cover Illustration: Esther Diana García

Illustrations: Carles Arbat Serarols pp. 152-163, 183; José Luis Briseño Sánchez pp. 179, 183; Esther Diana García pp. 10-17, 112-123, 181; María Lydia Lavezzi pp. 94-97, 102, 103; Luis Alberto Montiel Villegas pp. 76-85, 181; José Luis Navarro García pp. 26-33, 177; María Eugenia Nobati pp. 132-143; Pablo Sebastián Pino pp. 42-49, 58-66, 74, 179; Carlos Vélez Aguilera pp. 98-103

Photographs: © **AFP:** A.H.M REZWAN / AFP pp. 34-35, TOI PHOTOGRAPHER / THE TIMES OF INDIA p. 124 (bottom), ALEXANDER NEMENOV / AFP p. 125 (top), STRDEL / AFP p. 125 (bottom), HEIKO WOLFRAUM / DPA / DPA PICTURE-ALLIANCE p. 126 (bottom), WAKIL KOHSAR / AFP p. 127 (top), FARSHAD USYAN / AFP p. 127 (bottom), WAKIL KOHSAR / AFP p. 128 (left bottom), ANTOINE LORGNIER / ONLY WORLD / ONLY FRANCE p. 166 (top right), JEAN-JACQUES PANGRAZI / BIOSPHOTO p. 167 (top); © **Depositphotos.com:** UDMURD p. 164 (view through the window of Warsaw, Poland); © **Gettyimages.com:** Danny Iacob (back cover)

Images used under license from © **Depositphotos.com,** © **Shutterstock.com,** © **Stock.adobe.com**

Printed in Mexico by

Corporativo Prográfico S.A de C.V.
Calle Dos Núm. 257, Bodega 4,Col. Granjas San Antonio,
C.P. 09070 Del. Iztapalapa, Mexico, Mexico city.
in April 2019.

Reviewers

María Inés Curbelo
Clifton College
El Pinar, Uruguay

Miriam Durán
St. Michael's College
Adrogué, Buenos Aires, Argentina

Ana Inés Luciani Morlan
Life School
Montevideo, Uruguay

Ana Beatriz Medeiros de Sousa
Colégio Liessin
Rio de Janeiro, Brazil

Liziane Paiz Petri
Passo Certo Growing
Cascavel, Brazil

Sarah Robertson Yener
TED Antalya College
Antalya, Turkey

Jorge Torres Vera
Colegio Nuevo Hidalgo
Pachuca, Mexico

Jessica Véliz de Jordán
Colegio Metropolitano
Guatemala City, Guatemala

Engin Yılgın
Private Seymen High School
Izmit, Turkey

Scope and Sequence

Topic	Story / Text	Reading Strategies	Key Words	Connections
1 What English do I know? *Pages 9-24*	**Marco's First Day** by Robert Hill *Pages 10-17*	• **Identifying Characters**	first, good, happy, sad, say, think	**Connect to Geography** *Page 24*
	My Backpack by Suzanne Harris *Pages 18-23*	• **Using Pictures**	backpack, lunch, notebook, pencil, pencil case, storybook	
2 What's in my school? *Pages 25-40*	**Kroll the Trelf** by Deirdre Sullivan *Pages 26-33*	• **Details in the Poem**	behave, bridge, broom, gold, rule, yak	**Connect to Social Studies** *Page 40*
	Schools Around the World by Esther Mizrachi *Pages 34-39*	• **Main Idea and Details**	boat, high, mountain, noisy, train station, wet	
3 What's for lunch? *Pages 41-56*	**Lunch in the Garden** by Robert Hill *Pages 42-49*	• **Identifying Place**	eat, garden, hungry, pepper, pull, run	**Connect to Health** *Page 56*
	Let's Eat! by Suzanne Harris *Pages 50-55*	• **Comparing and Contrasting**	cinnamon, cook, mix, peanut butter, put, slice	
4 What do I like? *Pages 57-74*	**Singing Star** by Kelly Bingham *Pages 58-67*	• **Identifying Dialogue**	bark, birthday, dance, hear, shy, sing	**Connect to Social Studies** *Page 74*
	Toys Around the World by Esther Mizrachi *Pages 68-73*	• **Captions**	doll, drum, horse, loud, puppet, soft	
5 Who are my friends and family? *Pages 75-92*	**My Little Sister** by Debbie Thomas *Pages 76-85*	• **Central Message**	afraid, fence, hug, shout, stop, wag	**Connect to Social Studies** *Page 92*
	Twins! by Robert Hill *Pages 86-91*	• **Retelling**	born, identical, same, similar, sometimes, twin	

Topic Walkthrough

How to use my Reading Log

Think about the **Big Question** while you read.

There is a **fiction** story...

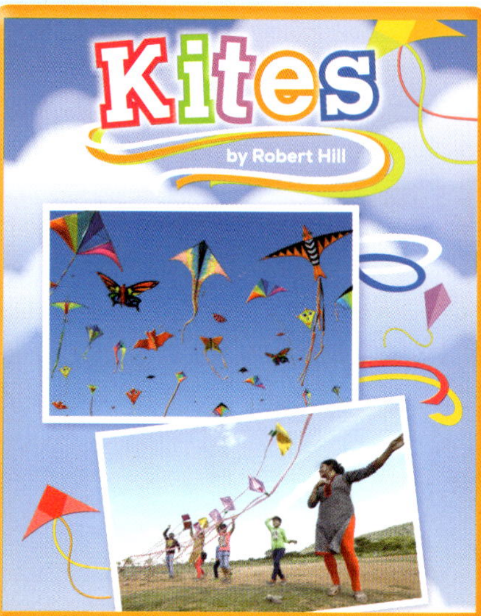

...and a **nonfiction** text for every topic.

Key Words help you understand the story.

Listen while you read.

Colorful pictures help tell the story.

Check your understanding with **Comprehension** activities.

Reading strategy activities help you become a better reader.

Comprehension

1 Listen and follow again. Match the parts of the sentences.

1 Mara is...
2 Mara lives...
3 A Selkie...
4 Mara likes...
5 Mara plays...
6 Mara doesn't like...

a the children's food.
b a Selkie.
c with the children.
d in the sea.
e to play games.
f is a Seal-Girl.

2 Read the words. Circle the correct pictures.

1 seal
2 bright
3 tickle
4 dry
5 whisker
6 change into

122 | Topic 7

3 **Identifying Sensory Words** Complete the sentences.

apple bright children sand sandwich

1 Mara sees... the ________ sun.
2 Mara hears... happy ________.
3 Mara feels... soft ________.
4 Mara tastes... a dry ________.
5 Mara tastes... a sweet ________.

+ Look and say. What else can Mara hear?

4 **Active Reading** Cut out the pictures on page 181. Attach each picture to an ice pop stick.

+ Listen and follow again. What descriptions do you hear? Hold up the pictures.

5 Think and d... ...a similar to the children? How is she different?

Selkie Girl | 123

Have more fun with the story in **Active Reading.**

Making Connections activities help you answer the **Big Question.**

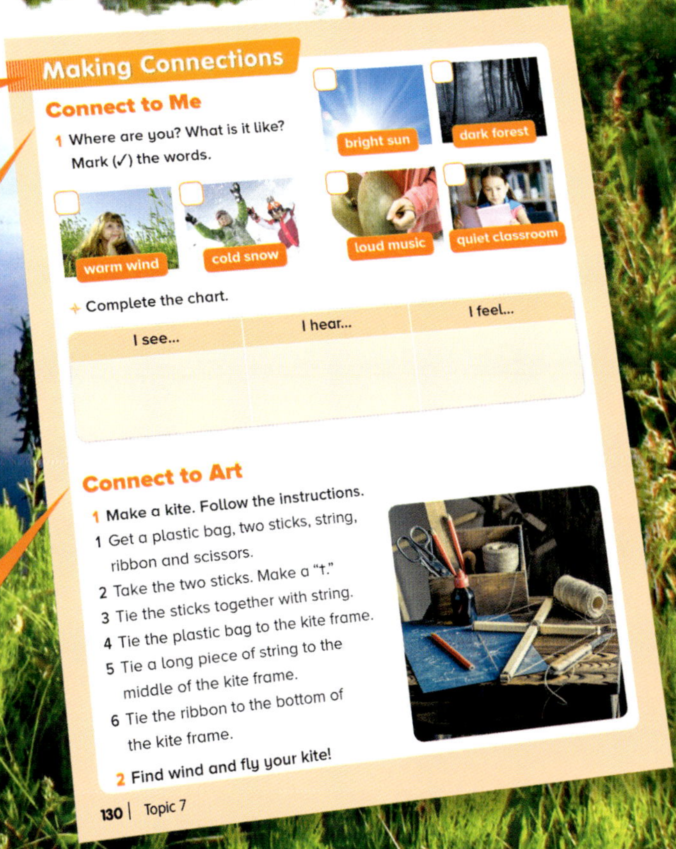
Making Connections

Connect to Me

1 Where are you? What is it like? Mark (✓) the words.

+ Complete the chart.

I see...	I hear...	I feel...

Connect to Art

1 Make a kite. Follow the instructions.
1 Get a plastic bag, two sticks, string, ribbon and scissors.
2 Take the two sticks. Make a "t."
3 Tie the sticks together with string.
4 Tie the plastic bag to the kite frame.
5 Tie a long piece of string to the middle of the kite frame.
6 Tie the ribbon to the bottom of the kite frame.

2 Find wind and fly your kite!

130 | Topic 7

With **Connect to Me**, you think about how the **Big Question** relates to you.

Think about the **Big Question** and your other school subjects.

Featured Authors

Kelly Bingham lives in Georgia, USA, with her family. Before she started writing children's books, she worked at Walt Disney Feature Animation as an artist and a film director. Kelly is the author of the award-winning books *Shark Girl, Z is for Moose,* and *Circle, Square, Moose.*

Kenn Nesbitt is a prize-winning poet. He is the author of many books, including *Kiss, Kiss Good Night, My Hippo Has the Hiccups* and *Revenge of the Lunch Ladies*. Visit his website, www.poetry4kids.com/, to read more of his poetry. It is the most visited children's poetry website on the Internet.

Deirdre Sullivan is a writer and teacher from Galway, Ireland. She writes books for teenagers, and scary stories for younger readers. Her third novel, *Primperfect* was shortlisted for the European Union Prize for Literature in 2015. She likes guinea pigs, reading and ghost stories.

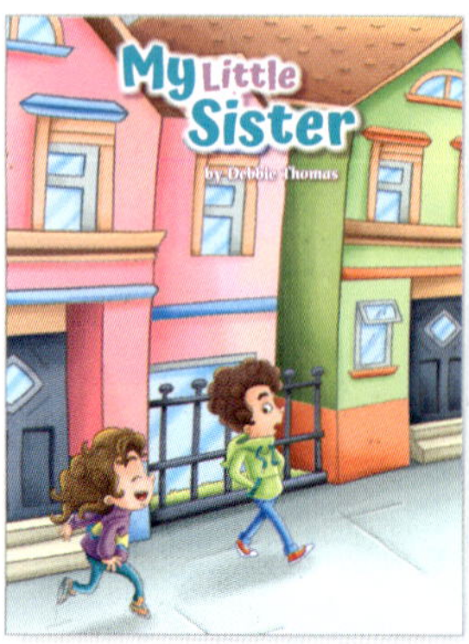

Debbie Thomas studied medicine and geology and then worked as a BBC radio journalist. Debbie now lives near Dublin and is the Writer in Residence at Crumlin Children's Hospital. She also writes and runs workshops for children across the country. She is known for her comedy adventure trilogy *Dead Hairy, Jungle Tangle* and *Monkie Business,* and *Class Act*. You can visit her at: debbie-thomas.com/.

Topic 1

What English do I know?

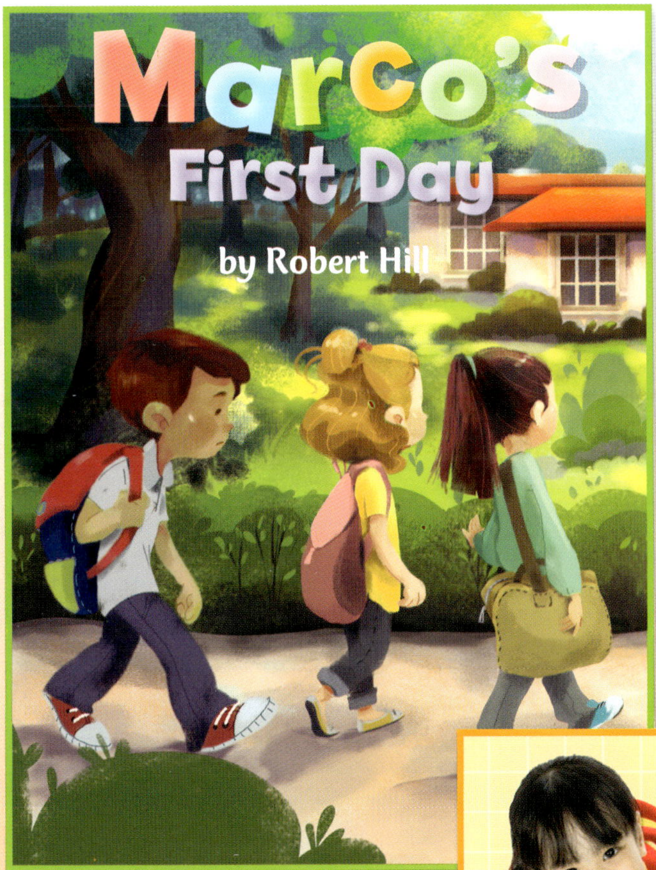

Marco's First Day

by Robert Hill

Key Words

first
good
happy
sad
say
think

1 Point to the boy. Who is he?

2 Listen and follow. 2

It is the **first** day of school.

Marco is **sad**.

*My English is not **good**!* he **thinks**.

"Hello!" **says** a girl.

"Hello," says Marco.

"I'm Anna! Who are you?"

"I'm Marco."

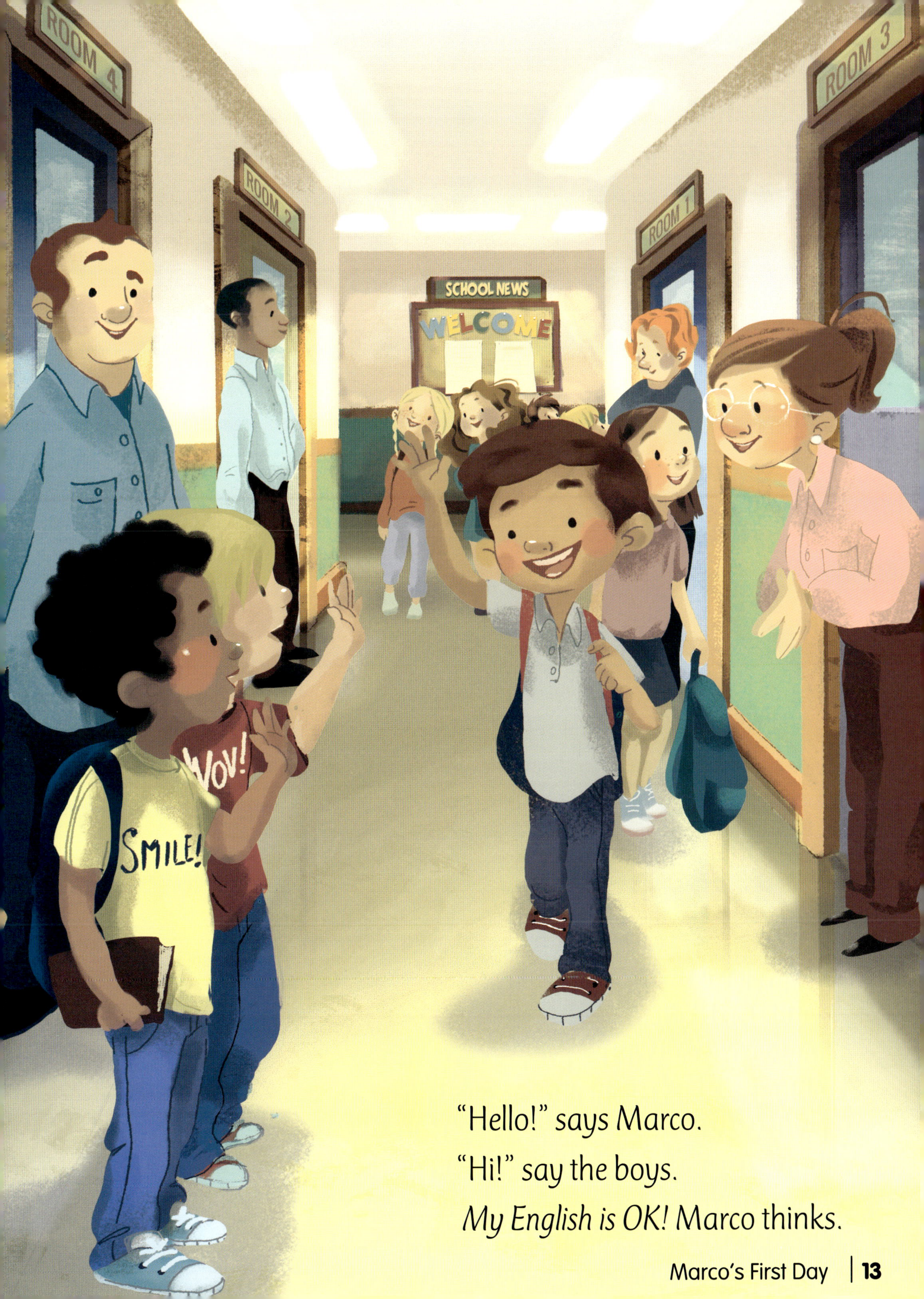

"Hello!" says Marco.

"Hi!" say the boys.

My English is OK! Marco thinks.

One, two, three! My room is number three! Marco thinks.

"Hello! Are you Marco?" asks the teacher.

"Yes, I am."

"I'm Ms. Baker. Welcome to our school!"

“This is your chair, Marco,” says the teacher.

Marco is **happy** now!

Wow! My English is good! he thinks.

Comprehension

1 Identifying Characters Listen and follow again. Mark (✓) the people in the story. 2

Anna	Marco	Ms. Baker

✦ Match the people with their names.

2 Circle the correct pictures.

1 Marco is sad.

2 Marco is happy.

3 "Welcome to our school!"

3 **Number the pictures in the correct order.**

4 **Read the question. Circle the correct answer.**

Why is Marco sad?

a He has a chair.

b He is in Room 3.

c He thinks his English is not good.

5 **Active Reading** **Cut out the pictures on page 175. Attach each picture to an ice pop stick.**

✧ **Listen and follow again. Hold up the happy or sad face.** 2

6 **Read and answer.**

What new English words do you know?

....

....

....

My Backpack

by Suzanne Harris

Key Words

backpack
lunch
notebook
pencil
pencil case
storybook

China

Hello! I'm Min.
I'm from China.
My **backpack** is
red and yellow.

What's in my backpack?

A **pencil case**.

1 Say the key words.
Point to the pictures.

2 Listen and follow. 3

Hi! I'm Mateo. I'm from Peru. My backpack is blue, yellow and red.

What's in my backpack?

A **notebook** and a **pencil**.

France

What's in my backpack?

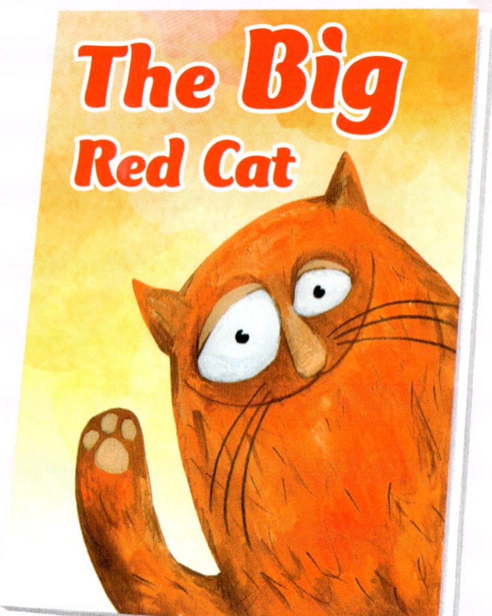

A **storybook**.

Hi. I'm Max. I'm from Canada. My backpack is blue.

What's in my backpack?

My **lunch**! Yum!

Comprehension

1 Listen and follow again. Complete their names. 3

1 
2 
3 
4 

M.......n M.......t....... .... G......... ....y M.........x

2 Using Pictures Cut out the pictures on page 175. Paste the pictures in the correct boxes.

1 What's in Min's backpack?

3 What's in Gaby's backpack?

2 What's in Mateo's backpack?

4 What's in Max's backpack?

3 Match the pictures with the words.

1

2

3

backpack

lunch

notebook

pencil

pencil case

storybook

4

5

6

4 **Active Reading** Listen and follow again. Clap when you hear a key word. 3

5 Think and draw. What's in your backpack?

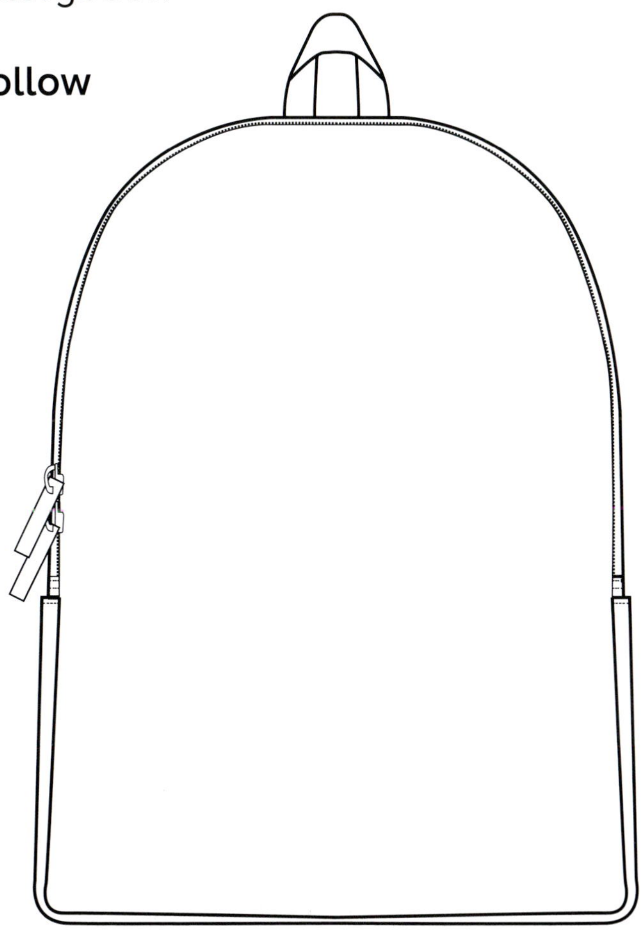

Making Connections

Connect to Me

1 Make your T-shirt.
Draw a picture.

Connect to Geography

1 Listen and follow. Complete the names of the countries. 4

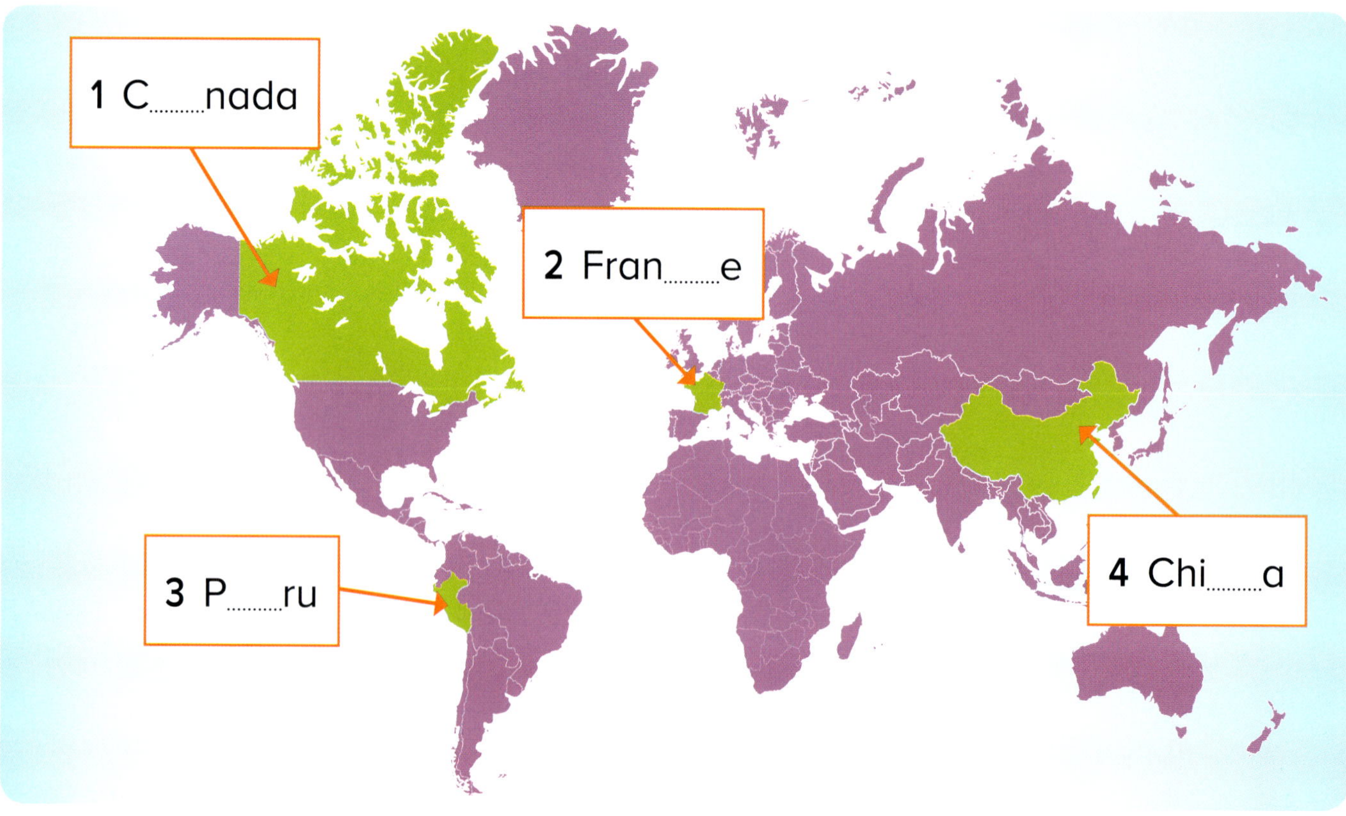

Topic 2

What's in my school?

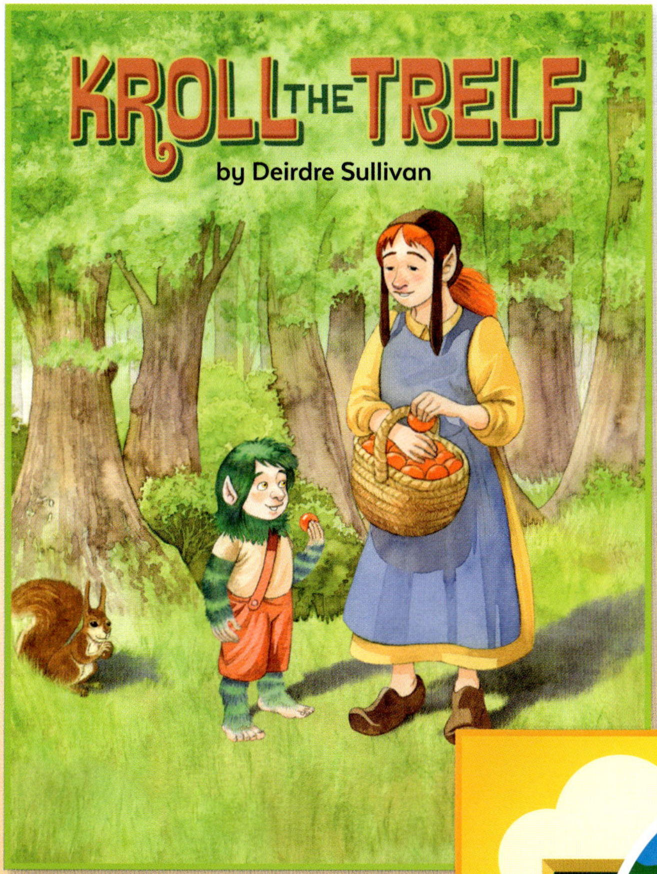

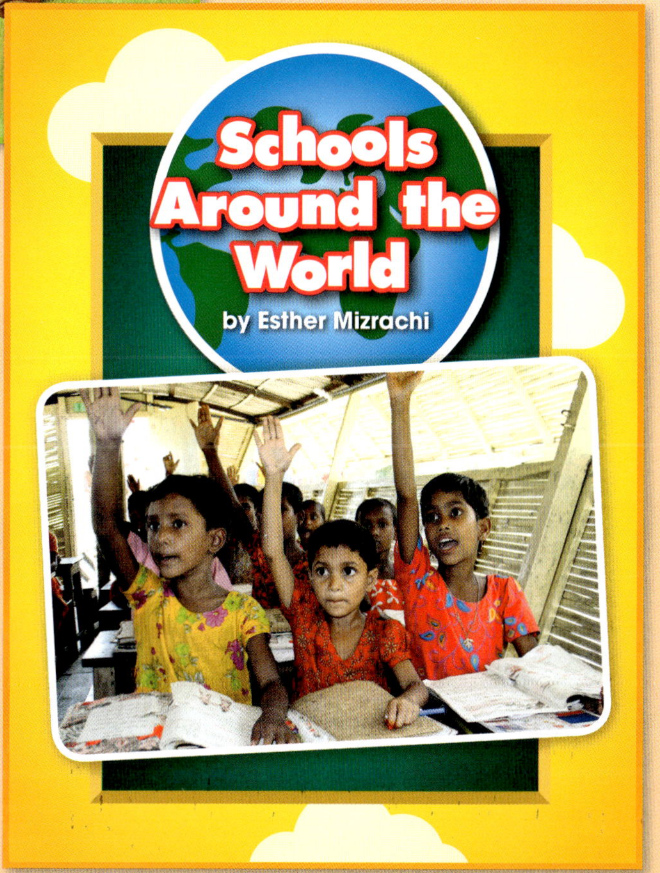

Key Words

behave
bridge
broom
gold
rule
yak

KROLL THE TRELF

by Deirdre Sullivan

1 Look at the picture. What's the poem about?

2 Listen and follow. 5

Hi! What's your name? My name is Kroll.
My mom's an elf, but my dad's a troll.
How old are you? I'm six years old.
My hair is green. My eyes are **gold**.

Where's your school? Under a **bridge**.
My teacher's nice. Her name is Midge.

What's in your backpack?

A pencil. A ruler. And a little **yak**.

What's his name? His name is Dave.

He's here to see that I **behave**.

What are the **rules** in Midge's room?

Be kind. Try hard. And fly your **broom**.

Your broom? My broom. It's like a bus.

But it only fits one of us.

You are funny, Kroll the Trelf.

Am I? I'm glad. I like myself.

I like you, too. Please be my friend.

Of course I will! And that's ... THE END!

Comprehension

1 **Listen and follow again. Complete their names.** 5

1

2

3

..........roll

..........idge

..........ave

She's a teacher.

He's a yak.

He's a student.

Match the characters with the descriptions.

2 **Complete the words. What's a *trelf*?**

1

2

3

Dad is a ....oll.

Mom is an ....lf.

Kroll is a tr.......... ....

3 **Details in the Poem** **Circle the correct words.**

1 Kroll is six / seven years old.

2 Kroll's mom / dad is a troll.

3 His hair is red / green.

4 His eyes are blue / gold.

Color the picture of Kroll.

4 Circle the correct pictures.

1 gold

a 

b 

2 bridge

a 

b 

3 behave

a 

b 

4 broom

a 

b 

5 yak

a 

b 

6 rule

a 

b 

5 Details in the Poem Look and circle. What's in Kroll's backpack?

a 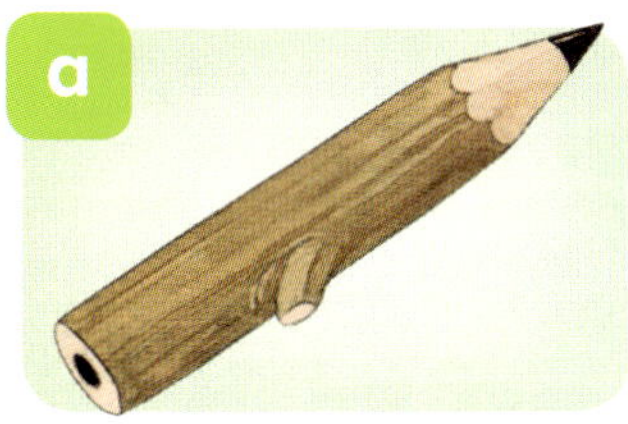

b 

c 

d 

6 Active Reading Cut out the pictures on page 177. Attach each picture to an ice pop stick.

✧ Listen and follow again. Hold up the characters when you hear their names. 5

7 Think and draw. What do you like about your school?

Key Words

boat
high
mountain
noisy
train station
wet

Schools Around the World

by Esther Mizrachi

1 Look at the title and pictures. What's the text about?

2 Listen and follow. 6

Let's visit some schools.

Boat School

Where is this school?

It's on a **boat**.

Careful! Sometimes it's **wet**.

Comprehension

1 Listen and follow again. Circle *Yes* or *No*. 6

1 There is a school on a boat. Yes No

2 There is a school on a plane. Yes No

3 There is a school on a mountain. Yes No

2 Match the words with the pictures.

1 boat

2 high

3 mountain

4 noisy

5 train station

6 wet

a

b

c

d

e

f

3 Main Idea and Details **Complete the sentences with the correct words.**

high	noisy	wet

1 The school on the boat is sometimes ....

2 The school at the train station is ....

3 The school on the mountain is .... up.

4 Active Reading **Listen and follow again. Act out the places.** 6

5 Look at the schools in the text. Draw a picture of your favorite school.

Making Connections

Connect to Me

1 Mark (✓) the rules in your school.

Look and listen

Try hard

Raise your hand

Sit quietly

Ask for help

Work together

Stand in line

Be kind

Connect to Social Studies

1 Where is a fun place to have a school?

....

....

....

....

....

2 Draw a picture of it.

What's for lunch?

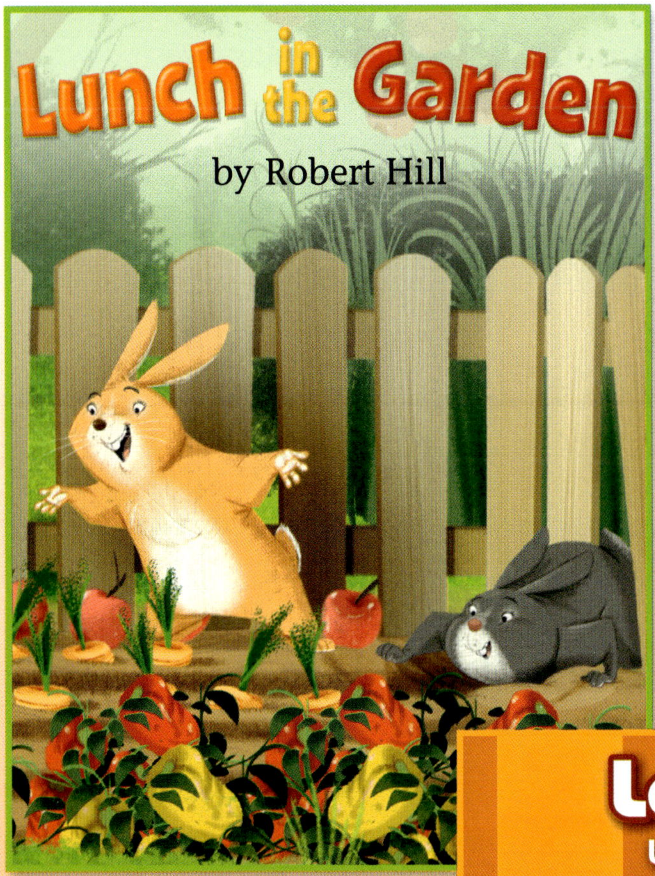

Lunch in the Garden

by Robert Hill

Key Words

eat
garden
hungry
pepper
pull
run

1 Look at the picture. Where are they?

2 Listen and follow. 7

Emma and Lucy go into a **garden**.
"Look, Lucy," says Emma. "Carrots! **Peppers**! Tomatoes!"
"And a lot of apples!" says Lucy.

"I'm **hungry**," says Emma.

She **eats** an apple and a carrot.

"I'm very hungry!" says Lucy.

She eats two apples and three carrots.

Emma eats a red pepper and a yellow pepper.

"I'm very hungry!" says Lucy.

She eats two red peppers, three yellow peppers and a tomato!

“Oh, no! Look! A man!” says Emma. “**Run**!”

Emma runs. Lucy runs. The man runs!

Emma goes out of the garden.

But Lucy…

Oh, no!

“**Pull**, Emma!” says Lucy. “Pull!”

Emma pulls and pulls…

POP!

“Oh, thank you, Emma!” says Lucy.

Key Words

cinnamon
cook
mix
peanut butter
put
slice

Let's Eat!

by Suzanne Harris

Peanut Butter and Jelly Sandwich

1 Look at the pictures. What do you see?

2 Listen and follow. 8

Let's make a **peanut butter** and jelly sandwich!

You need **bread**, **peanut butter** and **jelly**.

 +  + 

Step 1

Put peanut butter on a **slice** of bread.

Step 2

Put jelly on the other slice!

Step 3

Put the slices of bread together. Yum!

French Toast

You can make French toast!

You need **bread**, **eggs** and **cinnamon**.

Step 1

Mix the eggs and cinnamon.

Step 2

Put a slice of bread in the eggs.

Step 3

Cook the French toast. Yum!

Comprehension

1 **Listen and follow again. Mark (✓) the correct foods.** 8

☐ a sandwich ☐ a salad ☐ French toast

2 **Complete the words.**

1

co.........k

4

sl.........ce

2

p.........anut b.........tter

5

mi.........

3

p.........t

6

cin.........amon

3 Comparing and Contrasting Read the text. Match the ingredients with the foods.

1 cinnamon

2 peanut butter

3 eggs

4 bread

5 jelly

✧ Circle the ingredient in both recipes.

4 Active Reading Listen and follow again. Act out the steps. 8

5 Think and draw. What's your favorite food?

Making Connections

Connect to Me

1 Think and draw. What are your favorite vegetables?

Connect to Health

1 Look at the ingredients for a fruit salad. Circle the fruits you like.

apple

banana

grapes

strawberries

✦ Listen to the instructions. Number the steps in the correct order. 9

- ☐ Cut slices of apple, banana and strawberries.
- ☐ Put the fruit in a bowl.
- ☐ Eat your fruit salad. Yum!
- ☐ Wash the fruit.

Topic 4

What do I like?

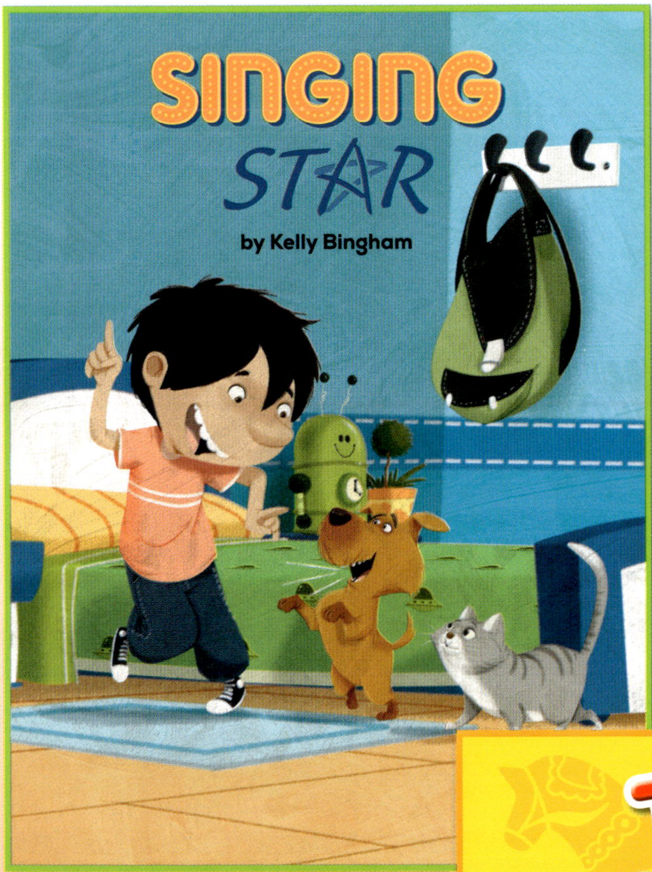

Key Words

bark
birthday
dance
hear
shy
sing

SINGING STAR

by Kelly Bingham

1 Find names and quotation marks. Who speaks in the story?

2 Listen and follow. 10

I am Alex.

I like to **sing**!

I like to **dance**!

I sing to my dog, Gizmo.

I sing to my cat, Lola.

Gizmo **barks**!

Mom **hears** us.

Mom dances!

"Very good!" says Mom.

"Thank you," I say.

Someday, I want to sing for many people.

But not now.

Now I sing only to Gizmo, Lola and Mom.

My sister Ana and her friend Emily are playing with their dolls.

"Sing to our dolls, please!" Ana says.

I don't want to sing to the dolls. I am **shy**.

"Please?" asks Emily.

I sing to the dolls.

I dance for them, too.

Emily dances with me.

It is fun!

"My **birthday** is tomorrow. Will you sing at my party?" Emily asks.

"Sing? For many people?" I ask.

"Alex, you can sing for many people!" says Ana. "You can do it!"

"Yes," I tell Emily. "I will sing at your party."

"Hooray!" The girls dance again.

I'm very happy!

TOYS AROUND THE WORLD

by Esther Mizrachi

Key Words

doll
drum
horse
loud
puppet
soft

My name is Elsa.
I'm from Sweden.
I like **horses**.
My Dala horse is
red and yellow.

Elsa's favorite toy

1 Look at the pictures.
What is the text about?

2 Listen and follow. 11

My name is Luca.
I'm from Italy.
I like **puppet** shows.
My puppet has strings.

Luca's favorite toy

My name is Davu.
I'm from Mali.
I like **drums**.
My djembe drum is **loud**.

My name is Rosa.
I'm from Mexico.
I like **dolls**.
My Maria doll is **soft**.

Rosa's favorite toy

Comprehension

1 Listen and follow again. Match the children with their countries. 11

1

2

3

4

2 Complete the words.

1

2

3

4

d.................................. p.................................. d.................................. h..................................

Circle the soft toy in red. Circle the loud toy in blue.

3 Captions Read the captions in the text. What are the objects? Circle the correct answer.

1 They are animals.

2 They are toys.

3 They are dolls.

4 Active Reading Color and cut out the pictures on page 179. Attach each picture to an ice pop stick.

✧ Listen and follow again. Hold up the correct toys when you hear them. 11

5 Think and draw. What toy do you like?

Making Connections

Connect to Me

1 Think about a party. Mark (✓) the activities you like to do.

Connect to Social Studies

1 Think about a traditional toy in your country. Draw a picture of it.

Who are my friends and family?

My Little Sister

by Debbie Thomas

Key Words

afraid
fence
hug
shout
stop
wag

1 Look at the pictures. What are the children doing?

2 Listen and follow. 12

My name is Ben. I'm eight. My sister Sally is six. We have brown eyes and curly brown hair. I like walking. She likes jumping. I like talking. She likes **shouting**. She loves dogs. I am **afraid** of them.

Today we are going to the shop. On the way, we hear a dog bark. I see the dog at a **fence**. I **stop** walking.

Sally walks up to the fence.
It's Spot. He is the neighbor's dog.
Spot barks.
"Shh..." she says.
Spot barks again.

"I said SHH, Spot!" Sally shouts.

"My brother is afraid of you."

She **wags** her finger. Spot stops barking.

He wags his tail. Spot likes Sally.

Sally puts her arms through the fence.
She **hugs** Spot.
"See, Ben?" she says. "He is nice.
Come and hug him."

I walk up to the fence. I do not hug Spot.
But I hug my sister.
"Thanks for helping me, Sally."

At the shop, I buy chocolate for Sally and a toy bone for Spot. But I will let Sally *give* Spot the bone.

Comprehension

1 **Listen to the first part of the story again. Match the descriptions with the characters.** 12

1 eight years old
2 six years old
3 likes walking
4 likes jumping

5 likes talking
6 likes shouting
7 loves dogs
8 is afraid of dogs

2 **Listen and follow again. Number the pictures in the correct order.** 12

Ben hugs Sally.

Spot barks.

Sally wags her finger.

Sally gives Spot the toy bone.

Spot stops barking.

Ben buys Sally chocolate.

3 Complete the words.

1

h........ ....

2

....op

3

sh........ ....t

4

f........n........e

5

w........ ....

6

af........ ....d

4 Central Message Circle the correct words. What can we learn from the story?

1 It's OK / not OK to be different. ☐

2 Sisters and brothers help / don't help each other. ☐

3 People say / don't say thank you. ☐

✧ **Mark (✓) the sentence that shows the central message for you.**

5 Active Reading Cut out the pictures on page 181. Attach each picture to an ice pop stick.

✧ **Listen and follow again. Hold up the characters when they speak or bark.** 12

6 Think about the story. Answer the questions.

1 Who is your favorite character? ....

2 Why? ....

✧ **Share your ideas with a classmate.**

Key Words

born
identical
same
similar
sometimes
twin

Twins!

by Robert Hill

Twins have
the **same** mother.
They are **born**
at the same time.

They have the
same birthday.

1 Look at the pictures. How many girls are there? How many boys?

2 Listen and follow. 13

Twins are **similar**.
But they are not
the same.

Sometimes twins
are sisters.

Sometimes they
are brothers.

Sometimes they
are a brother
and a sister.

Making Connections

Connect to Me

1 Look at the pictures.
What are you afraid of?

✧ Think and discuss. What can you do when you are afraid? What can you do when a friend is afraid?

Connect to Social Studies

1 Draw a picture of a family member who looks like you.

✧ Think and write. How are you similar?

....

....

....

....

....

....

....

....

What am I good at?

SILA'S PAINTBRUSH

by Esther Mizrachi

Key Words

cow
farmer
grow
paintbrush
plant
river

1 Look at the pictures. Where are they?

2 Listen and follow. 14 and 15

Sila has a magic **paintbrush**.

I can help people, she thinks.

"I need water," a farmer says. "My **plants** do not **grow**."

Sila paints a **river**. The **farmer** waters his plants. They grow and grow.

"Thank you, Sila," the farmer says.

He is happy. Sila is happy.

"We are hungry," a mother says.

Sila paints an apple tree. She paints chickens. She paints a **cow**. The family eats apples and eggs. They drink milk.

"Thank you, Sila," they say.

They are happy. Sila is happy.

Who can I help now? Sila thinks.

Sara's Pencil

by Esther Mizrachi

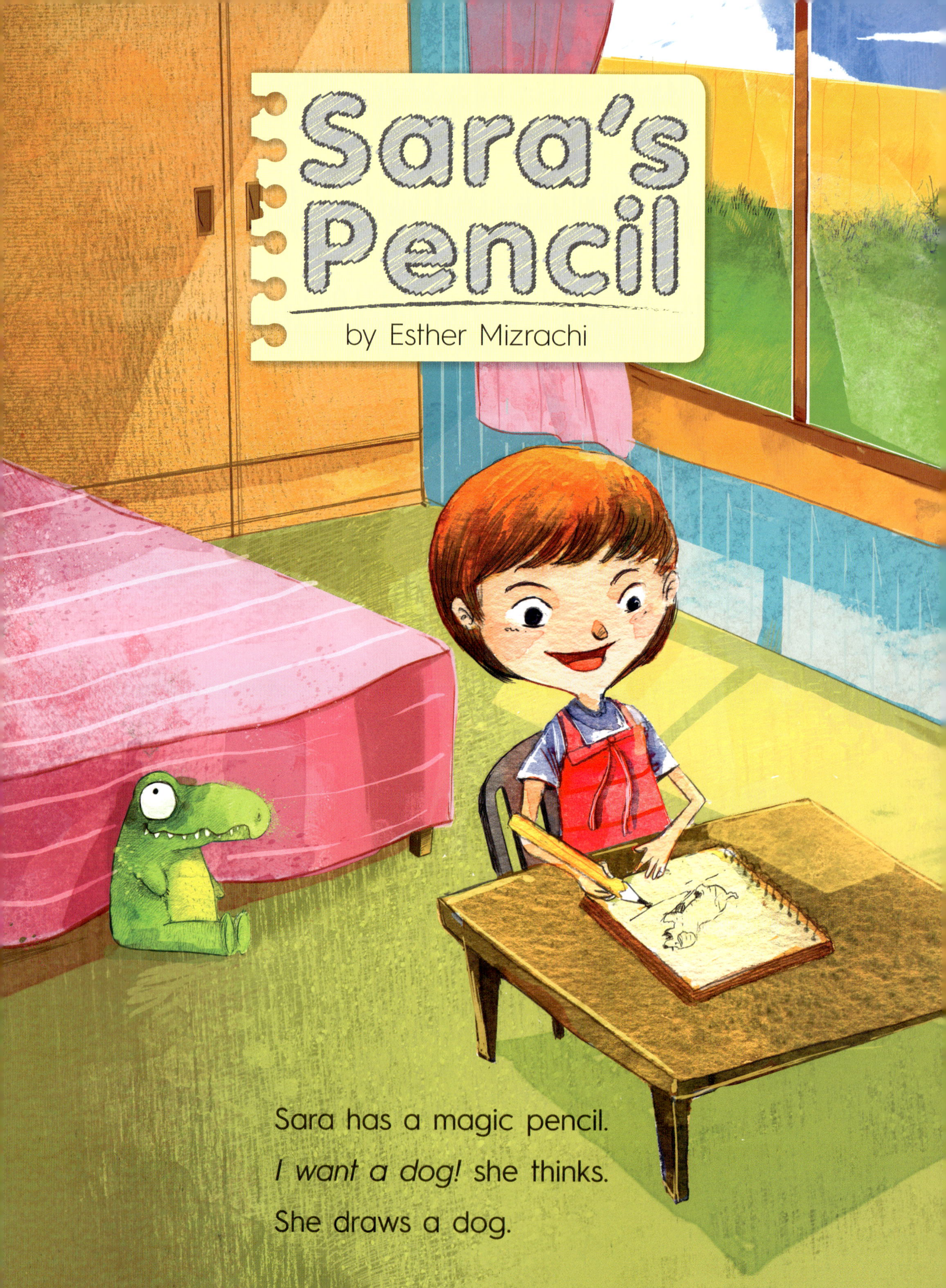

Sara has a magic pencil.

I want a dog! she thinks.

She draws a dog.

She looks around her room. She looks outside.

"Oh, no!" she shouts. "That's a very big dog!"

"Woof," says the dog.

Sara is not happy.

Sara sits and thinks.

"I want new shoes!" she says.

She draws shoes.

She looks around her room. She looks under the bed. She opens her closet.

"Oh, no!" she shouts. Sara is not happy.

Why can't I draw things I want? she thinks.

Key Words

beat
chess
everyone
jigsaw puzzle
picture
sell

What Children Can Do!

by Robert Hill

The Kay family is from Canada.
Everyone can play the piano!
Mom is a piano teacher.
Susan likes to play with her brother.

1 Look at the pictures on this page. What are they doing?

2 Listen and follow. 16

Ivan is from Russia.

He likes to play **chess**.

He can **beat** his classmates.

And he can beat his grandfather!

Camila is from Mexico.

Her favorite colors are yellow and blue.

She paints **pictures** with her sister.

They **sell** a lot of pictures!

The Lee family is from Australia.
They like to do **jigsaw puzzles**.
Mom and Dad are good at doing jigsaw puzzles.
But James and Lisa are very good!

Comprehension

1 Listen and follow again. Match the children with their countries. 16

1 Susan	Mexico
2 Ivan	Russia
3 Camila	Australia
4 James and Lisa	Canada

2 Complete the words.

1

a game of …… ……ess

2

a p……c……ur…… of flowers

3

eve…… ……on…… in their family

4

b…… ……t her dad in a video game

5

se…… …… lemonade

6

do a ……i……sa…… pu…… ……le

3 Read the questions. Circle the correct answers.

1 Who can play chess?

a Ivan b Susan

2 Who can do jigsaw puzzles?

a Camila b James and Lisa

3 Who can paint pictures?

a Ivan b Camila

4 Who can play the piano?

a Susan b James and Lisa

4 Describing the Connection Think about everyone in the text. What are they good at? Mark (✓) the answer.

- [ ] Everyone is good at playing a musical instrument.
- [ ] Everyone is good at games.
- [ ] Everyone is good at an activity.
- [ ] Everyone is good at painting pictures.

5 Active Reading Listen and follow again. Act out the actions when you hear them. 16

1 play the piano
2 play chess
3 paint pictures
4 do jigsaw puzzles

6 Think and draw. What activity do you do with your family?

Making Connections

Connect to Me

1 Think and draw. What are you good at? How can you help other people?

I am good at …………………………………….	I can help by …………………………………….

Connect to Art

1 **Follow the instructions to make a jigsaw puzzle.**

1 Draw and color a picture.
2 Cut the picture into pieces.
3 Exchange jigsaw puzzles with a classmate.
4 Put your classmate's jigsaw puzzle together!

Topic 7

What do children in other countries do?

Key Words

- bright
- change into
- dry
- seal
- tickle
- whisker

Selkie Girl

A story from Ireland

by Deirdre Sullivan

1 Look at the pictures. What can you see?

2 Listen and follow. 17

Mara is a Selkie.

She is the smallest Selkie in the sea.

Sometimes she is a **seal**.

Sometimes she is a girl.

She eats fish for breakfast.

She eats fish for lunch.

For dinner, she sometimes eats ... more fish.

Mara is happy. She likes to swim.

The water is wet on her skin.

She feels the sea **tickle** her **whiskers**.

One day, she hears children on the beach.

Mara swims closer.

They get louder and happier.

Mara likes to hear the children.

She likes to play games.

Mara comes out of the sea.

She **changes into** a girl.

She sees the **bright** sun.

She feels the soft sand under her feet.

"Hello Seal-Girl!" say the children.

Mara smiles at them.

"My name is Mara," she tells them.

They play ball and fly a kite.

Her friends get hungry.

They eat sandwiches and apples.

Mara tries a sandwich. It is too **dry**.

Mara tries an apple. It is too sweet.

In the evening, the sky is orange and pink.
Mara's friends are tired.
They go home to their dinners and their beds.
But Mara is home. Her home is the sea.
Her bed is made of water and sand.

She watches her friends running home.
Then, she goes to the sea.
She changes into a seal again.
Mara's father has a nice dinner ready.
It is fish. Mara smiles. Fish is good.

Comprehension

1 **Listen and follow again. Match the parts of the sentences.** 17

1 Mara is...
2 Mara lives...
3 A Selkie...
4 Mara likes...
5 Mara plays...
6 Mara doesn't like...

a the children's food.
b a Selkie.
c with the children.
d in the sea.
e to play games.
f is a Seal-Girl.

2 **Read the words. Circle the correct pictures.**

1 seal

a 

b 

2 bright

a 

b 

3 tickle

a 

b 

4 dry

a 

b 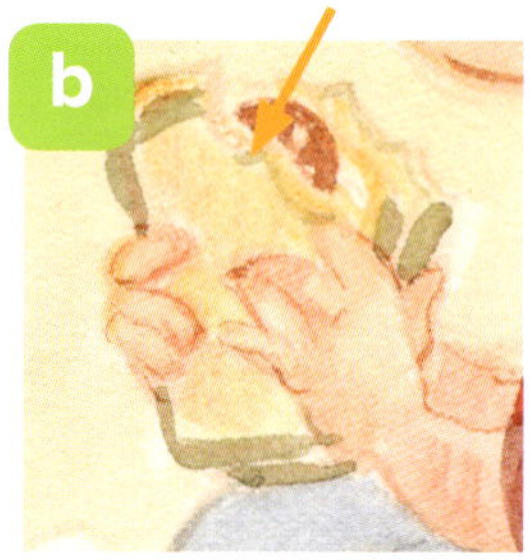

5 whisker

a 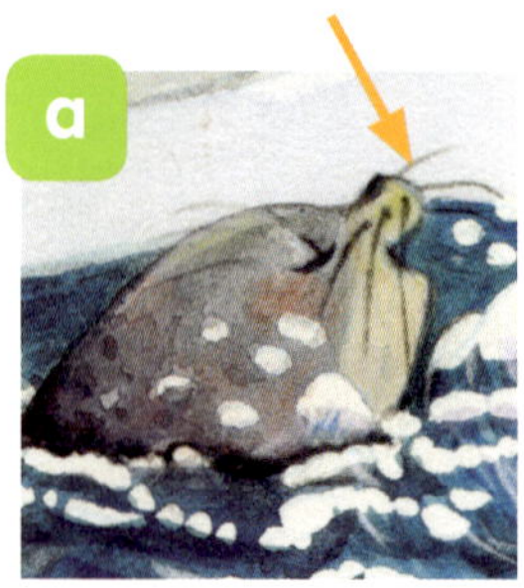

b 

6 change into

a 

b 

3 Identifying Sensory Words Complete the sentences.

apple bright children sand sandwich

1 Mara sees...

the .... sun.

2 Mara hears...

happy ....

3 Mara feels...

soft ....

4 Mara tastes...

a dry ....

5 Mara tastes...

a sweet ....

✧ Look and say. What else can Mara hear?

4 Active Reading Cut out the pictures on page 181. Attach each picture to an ice pop stick.

✧ Listen and follow again. What descriptions do you hear? Hold up the pictures. 17

5 Think and discuss. How is Mara similar to the children? How is she different?

Key Words
buy
cut
fight
market
sharp
string

Kites

by Robert Hill

Flying kites is popular in many countries.

Children like to play with kites.

And parents like to play, too!

1 Look at the pictures. What can you see?

2 Listen and follow. 18

Flying kites is very popular in Afghanistan. People **buy** kites in the **market**.
They also buy **string** for kites in the market.
The string is **sharp**!

Kite fighting is a popular game in Afghanistan.

Kite fighters **fight** with their kites!

The kites **cut** the strings of other kites with their sharp strings.

When they cut the strings, the kites fly away.

Kite runners run after these kites.

Sometimes they run three or four kilometers!

Making Connections

Connect to Me

1 Where are you? What is it like? Mark (✓) the words.

✧ Complete the chart.

I see...	I hear...	I feel...

Connect to Art

1 **Make a kite. Follow the instructions.**

1 Get a plastic bag, two sticks, string, ribbon and scissors.

2 Take the two sticks. Make a “t.”

3 Tie the sticks together with string.

4 Tie the plastic bag to the kite frame.

5 Tie a long piece of string to the middle of the kite frame.

6 Tie the ribbon to the bottom of the kite frame.

2 **Find wind and fly your kite!**

Topic 8

Where do animals live?

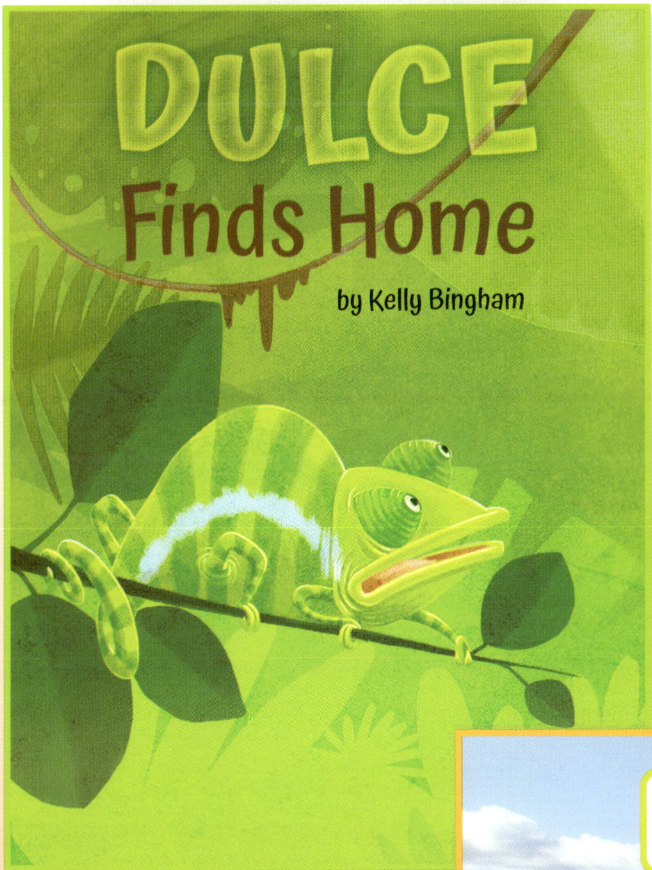

Key Words

branch
fast
log
lost
point
toe

DULCE Finds Home

by Kelly Bingham

1 Read the title and look at the pictures. Who is Dulce?

2 Listen and follow. 19

My name is Dulce. I am a chameleon.
Today I went for a walk. Now I am **lost**!
Where is my home?

"Where are you going?" asks an aye-aye.

"Home," I say. "It's in a **log**. Next to the river."

"Go that way," says the aye-aye. He **points**.
"Thank you." I walk on a **branch**. I use my **toes**.
I use my tail.

I see two blue couas.

Look! I can change colors!

Now I am blue, too!

"Hello!" I say.

"Where are you going?" ask the couas.

"Home. It's in a log. Next to the river," I say.

"That way!" say the couas. They point.

"Thank you."

I walk past two red frogs.

They have yellow eyes.

Now I am red and yellow, too!

"Where are you going?" asks a lemur.

"Home. It's in a log. Next to the river," I say.

"That way," says the lemur. She points.

"Thank you," I say. I walk **fast** now.

The sun is low. Birds fly by.
Night animals come out.
Oh, no! Hungry crocodiles!
I want to go home!

"Dulce?" asks a yellow moth. "Is that you?"
"Florita!" I say.
Florita is my friend. She lives next to me.
"I am lost!" I tell her.
"This way," says Florita.

Florita flies past flowers. I walk under them.

I hear water! I see the river! I see my log! I am home!

"Thank you!" I say. "Good night!"

I love my bed! I am safe at last. Time to sleep!

Comprehension

1 Listen and follow again. Number the pictures in the correct order. 19

I walk past two red frogs.

"This way," says Florita.

"Where are you going?" asks an aye-aye.

I am safe at last.

I see two blue couas.

"That way," says the lemur.

2 Complete the words.

1

t_____ _____

2

f_____ _____t

3

l_____g

4

l_____ _____t

5

p_____ _____nt

6

br_____ _____ch

3 Developing Visual Literacy Look at the pictures. Circle *Yes* or *No*.

1 The aye-aye helps Dulce.	Yes	No
2 The frogs help Dulce.	Yes	No
3 The crocodiles are friends.	Yes	No
4 The moth is walking fast.	Yes	No

✧ Color Dulce with the correct colors.

4 Active Reading Listen and follow again. Draw Dulce's path home. 19

✧ Complete the sentences. Where is Dulce's home?

It's in a .... Next to the ....

5 Think and discuss. Where is your home?

Key Words

alive
colony
root
saltwater
sunny
sunscreen

Let's Explore!

by Suzanne Harris

A Coral Reef

Look! A coral reef! There are reefs all around the world.

What is coral?
Rocks? No.
Plants? No.

1 Look at the pictures. What places and animals do you see?

2 Listen and follow. 20

Corals are very small animals. They are called *coral polyps*. They grow in big **colonies**.

Coral can be many colors. White coral isn't **alive**.

Some **sunscreen** is bad for coral. Always use zinc sunscreen.

Many fish, plants and animals need coral reefs.

A Mangrove Forest

A mangrove is a tree. It can live in **saltwater**. You can see its **roots**! Mangroves grow near the ocean. Most mangrove forests are in hot and **sunny** places.

Sea Turtle

Pelican

Alligator

Manatee

Heron

Mangrove forests are very important.
Many birds and animals live there.
Fish and insects live there, too.

Making Connections

Connect to Me

1 Look at the pictures. Mark (✓) the animals that live near you.

✦ What other animals live near you?

....

....

Connect to Life Science

1 Read the texts. Circle the Great Barrier Reef in orange. Circle the mangrove forests in green.

The Great Barrier Reef is in the Coral Sea. It is near Australia. There are 3,000 coral reefs there. The Great Barrier Reef is the same size as Italy or Japan.

Indonesia is a country with many islands. Mangrove trees grow around the islands. They protect the islands. Many animals live there.

Topic 9

What's happening at home?

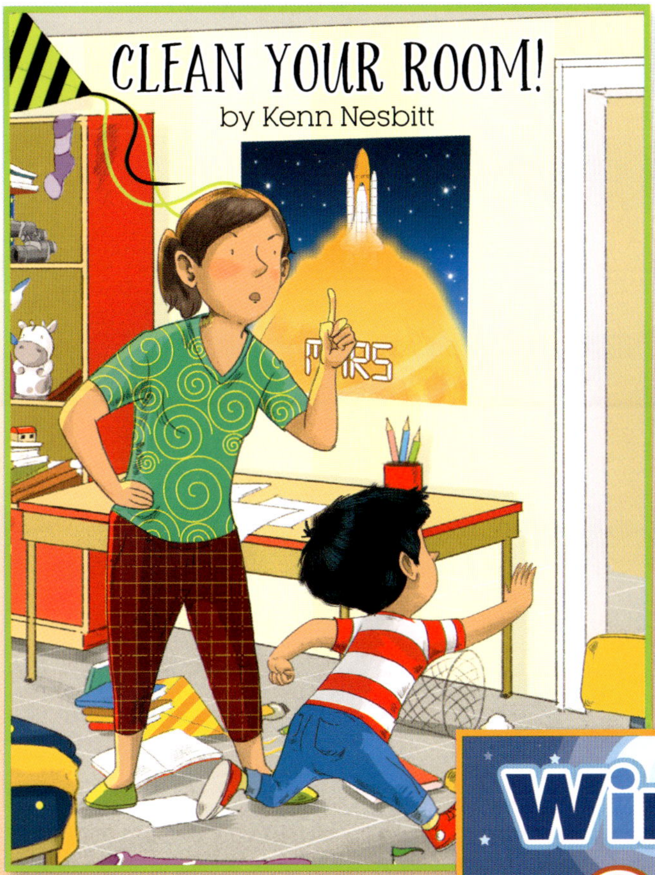

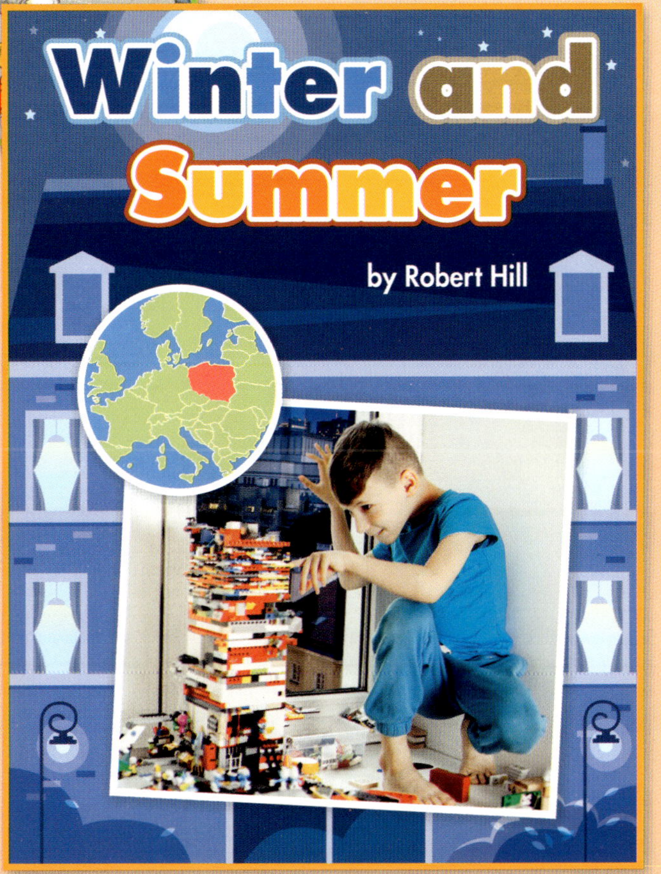

CLEAN YOUR ROOM!

by Kenn Nesbitt

Key Words

floor
mop
rag
slop
sweep
trash

1 Look at page 153. How many lines of text are there?

2 Listen and follow. 21

Your mother says to clean your room.
First, you need to find a broom.
You need a broom to clean the **floor**.
You are running out the door.

You are picking up the broom.
Now you throw it in your room.
The broom is flying at your bed.
Whoops! The cat! It hits his head!

You are looking for a **mop**.

It is good for cleaning **slop**.

There it is. Right over there.

In the kitchen, by a chair.

You are running to your room.
Now you throw the mop in with the broom.
It is flying and ... KERSPLAT!
Whoops! It also hits the cat!

Now you need to find a bag.

And you need a cleaning **rag**.

You are looking all around.

Here they are. You get them down.

You are running with the bag.
And you have the cleaning rag.
Then you throw them in your room.
Whoops! They hit the cat! KABOOM!

Now you go to clean your room.

It is time to use the broom.

You are looking from the door.

Your cat is **sweeping** up the floor!

He is cleaning up your room.

He can use a mop and a broom!

All your **trash** is in the bag.

He is cleaning with the rag.

He is very good at that.

Your cat is nice. You like your cat.

Your room is clean. You pet his head.

Now he is sleeping on your bed.

Comprehension

1 Identifying Rhyming Words Listen and follow again. Match the lines of the poem that rhyme. 21

1

Your mother says to clean your room.

2

You are looking for a mop.

3

You are looking all around.

4

You are looking from the door.

a

It is good for cleaning slop.

b

Your cat is sweeping up the floor!

c

First, you need to find a broom.

d

Here they are. You get them down.

2 **Complete the words.**

1 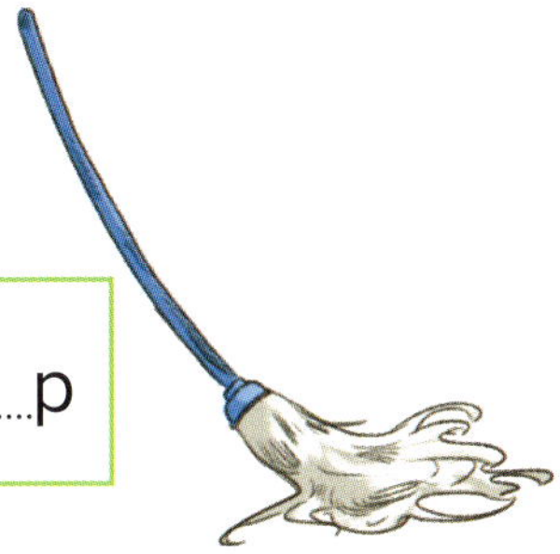

m.........p

2 

r.........g

3 

tr.........sh

4 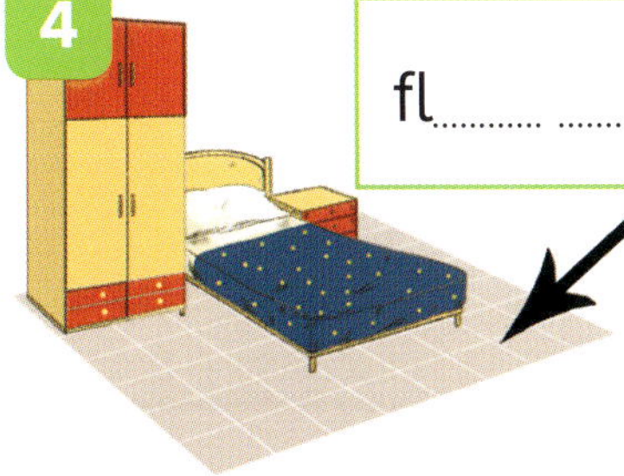

fl......... ....r

5 

sw......... ....p

6 

sl.........p

3 **Read the sentences. Circle the correct words.**

1 Your mother / brother says to clean your room.

2 The broom / mop is by a chair.

3 You need a broom / rag to clean the floor.

4 The boy / cat is cleaning the room.

4 **Active Reading Cut out the pictures on page 183. Attach each picture to an ice pop stick.**

✧ **Listen and follow again. Hold up the pictures when you hear the words.** 21

5 **Imagine you are the cat. Tell the story.**

Key Words

dark
light
park
stone
summer
winter

Winter and Summer

by Robert Hill

I'm Jakub from Warsaw, Poland.
In **winter**, the evenings are **dark**.
We have dinner at 5 o'clock.
Then I play with **building bricks**.

1 Look at the text. Point to the words in blue.

2 Listen and follow. 22

In **summer**, the evenings are **light**.

I play in the **park**.

We have dinner at 7 o'clock.

We like potato **pierogi**!

I'm Anka from Iqaluit, Canada.
In winter, it's dark at 2 o'clock!
I look for the **northern lights**.
We have dinner at 5 o'clock.
We like dried fish.

In summer, it's still light at 11 o'clock!
We have dinner at 7 o'clock.
Then I find **stones** and make **inuksuit**.

Comprehension

1 Listen and follow again. Circle *Yes* or *No*. 22

1	Jakub is from Portugal.	Yes	No
2	Jakub eats pierogi for dinner.	Yes	No
3	In winter, Jakub plays in the park.	Yes	No
4	Anka is from Canada.	Yes	No
5	Anka makes inuksuit.	Yes	No
6	Anka likes fish soup for dinner.	Yes	No

2 Match the words with the pictures.

a

1 dark

2 light

d

b

3 park

4 stone

e

c

5 summer

6 winter

f

3 Active Reading Listen and follow again. Point to the pictures of building bricks, pierogi, inuksuit and northern lights. 22

4 Using Picture Cues Find the words in blue in the text. Look at the pictures. Match the words with the descriptions.

1 building bricks
2 pierogi
3 northern lights
4 inuksuit

a They're colored lights.
b They're toys.
c They're sculptures.
d It's food.

5 Read the questions. Mark (✓) the answers.

Questions	Jakub	Anka
1 Who has dinner at 5 o'clock in the winter?	....	....
2 Who plays with building bricks?	....	....
3 Who looks for the northern lights?	....	....
4 Who makes inuksuit?	....	....
5 Who likes dried fish?	....	....
6 Who likes potato pierogi?	....	....

6 Think and draw. What do you do in the summer?

Making Connections

Connect to Me

1 **Circle the things to clean. What do you need to clean them?**

Connect to Social Studies

1 **Read about inuksuit.**

The Inuit people make inuksuit
to welcome visitors.
An inuksuk looks like a person.

2 **Make an inuksuk. Follow the instructions.**

1 Get 10 to 12 flat stones and a piece of cardboard.

2 Balance the stones on the cardboard, one on top of the other.

Glossary

Topic 1

Fiction

first (adj.) coming before all others in time, order or importance

good (adj.) able to do something well; skillful

happy (adj.) feeling full of joy

sad (adj.) feeling unhappy

say (v.) to express in words; to speak

think (v.) to use your mind

Nonfiction

backpack (n.) a bag with shoulder straps to carry school supplies

lunch (n.) the meal you eat in the middle of the day

notebook (n.) a small book of paper for notes

pencil (n.) an object for writing or drawing

pencil case (n.) a small container for carrying pencils and pens

storybook (n.) a book of stories for children

Topic 2

Fiction

behave (v.) to act in an appropriate way

bridge (n.) a structure that is built over something so that people can cross from one side to the other

broom (n.) a brush that has a long handle and is used for sweeping

gold (adj.) a deep yellow color

rule (n.) an instruction that tells you what you can or cannot do

yak (n.) a big animal with long hair and curved horns

Nonfiction

boat (n.) a small vehicle that is used for travel on water

high (adj.) far off the ground; very tall

mountain (n.) an area of land that rises high above the land around it

noisy (adj.) making loud sounds

train station (n.) a place where trains stop so that people can get on and off

wet (adj.) covered in water or another liquid; not dry

Topic 3

Fiction

eat (v.) to put into the mouth and swallow it

garden (n.) an area of land where herbs, fruits, flowers and vegetables grow

hungry (adj.) a feeling in the stomach because you need food

pepper (n.) a red, green, orange or yellow vegetable

pull (v.) to hold someone or something and move it toward you

run (v.) to move your legs quickly, faster than walking

Nonfiction

cinnamon (n.) a sweet spice that comes from the bark of a tree and is used in cooking and baking

cook (v.) to prepare food for eating by using heat

mix (v.) to combine two or more things

peanut butter (n.) a creamy food that is made from peanuts

put (v.) to place or move something to a different location

slice (n.) a thin piece of food that is cut from something bigger

Topic 4

Fiction

bark (v.) to make the short, loud sound of a dog

birthday (n.) the day someone is born

dance (v.) to move your body as music plays

hear (v.) to perceive sounds through the ears

shy (adj.) nervous or uncomfortable about meeting or talking to people

sing (v.) to use the voice to make musical sounds in the form of a song or tune

Nonfiction

doll (n.) a toy in the form of a baby or small person

drum (n.) a musical instrument with a thin layer of material on a round frame

horse (n.) a large animal that is used for riding and for carrying or pulling things

loud (adj.) making a lot of sound

puppet (n.) a doll that is moved by a hand or by strings

soft (adj.) easy to press, bend or cut; smooth and pleasant to touch

Topic 5

Fiction

afraid (adj.) scared; frightened

fence (n.) a structure like a wall, made of wood or metal that prevents people or animals from entering or leaving

hug (v.) to place arms around someone as a way to show affection and caring

shout (v.) to speak loudly

stop (v.) to not move

wag (v.) to move something from side to side repeatedly

Nonfiction

born (adj.) to come into life

identical (adj.) exactly like someone or something else

same (adj.) exactly like someone or something else

similar (adj.) almost the same as someone or something else

sometimes (adv.) at certain times; now and then

twin (n.) a child who is born at the same time as another child to the same mother

Topic 6

Fiction

cow (n.) a large animal that is raised by people for milk and meat

farmer (n.) a person who grows vegetables or fruit or raises animals

grow (v.) to come to life and develop; to get bigger

paintbrush (n.) a brush that is used to paint on something

plant (n.) a living thing that grows in the ground

river (n.) a large stream of moving water

Nonfiction

beat (v.) to win a game against another person or team

chess (n.) a board game for two players; each player has sixteen pieces that can be moved in different ways

everyone (n.) every person

jigsaw puzzle (n.) a game with small pieces of various shapes that fit together to form a picture

picture (n.) a painting, drawing or photograph

sell (v.) to give something to someone for money

Topic 7

Fiction

bright (adj.) full of light

change into (v.) to alter physical form

dry (adj.) not having the usual amount of moisture

seal (n.) a large animal that lives in the sea near coasts, has flippers and eats fish

tickle (v.) to touch a body part softly in order to cause a tingling feeling

whisker (n.) a long hair near the mouth of an animal

Nonfiction

buy (v.) to give money in exchange for something

cut (v.) to divide something with a sharp tool

fight (v.) to use objects to win a competition or beat a competitor

market (n.) a place where people buy and sell things

sharp (adj.) having a thin edge that can cut things

string (n.) a long, thin piece of twisted thread

Topic 8

Fiction

branch (n.) a part of a tree that grows out from the trunk

fast (adv.) at high speed

log (n.) the trunk of a tree that has fallen or been cut down

lost (adj.) not knowing where you are or how to get to where you want to go

point (v.) to show someone where to look or go

toe (n.) one of the five separate parts at the end of a foot

Nonfiction

alive (adj.) having life; not dead

colony (n.) a group of plants or animals living or growing in one place

root (n.) the part of the plant that grows underground or underwater, gets water and minerals, and holds the plant in place

saltwater (n.) water that naturally has salt in it

sunny (adj.) full of bright sunlight

sunscreen (n.) a lotion or spray you put on your skin to prevent sunburn

Topic 9

Fiction

floor (n.) the part of the room on which you stand

mop (n.) a tool for cleaning floors that has yarn or a sponge tied to a long stick

rag (n.) a piece of cloth

slop (n.) liquid spilled on a floor

sweep (v.) to remove dirt or dust with a broom or brush

trash (n.) something that is not useful or wanted

Nonfiction

dark (adj.) very little or no light

light (adj.) having the light of the sun

park (n.) an area of land, often in a city, that has grass, trees and other plants

stone (n.) a small piece of rock

summer (n.) a season of the year after spring and before fall, known for hot weather and longer days

winter (n.) a season of the year after fall and before spring, known for cold weather and snow

Topic 1 "Marco's First Day"

Topic 1 "My Backpack"

Topic 2 “Kroll the Trelf”

Cutouts

Topic 4 “Singing Star”

Topic 4 “Toys Around the World”

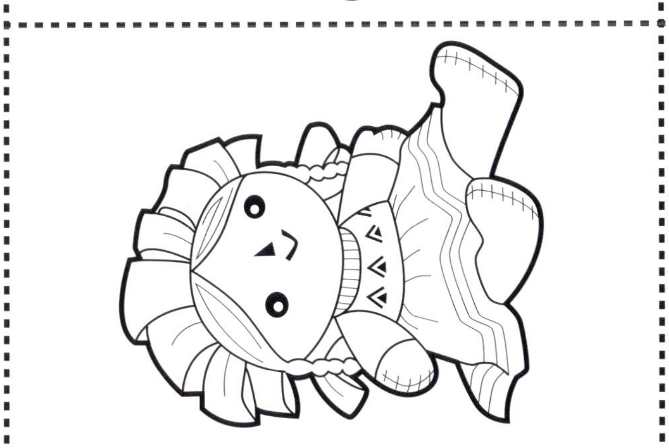

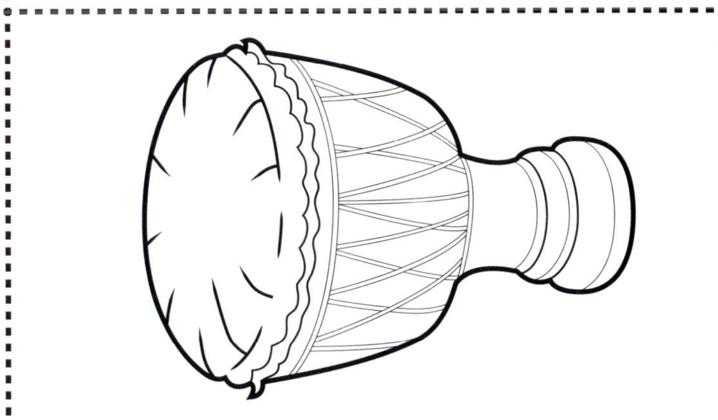

Topic 5 "My Little Sister"

Topic 7 "Selkie Girl"

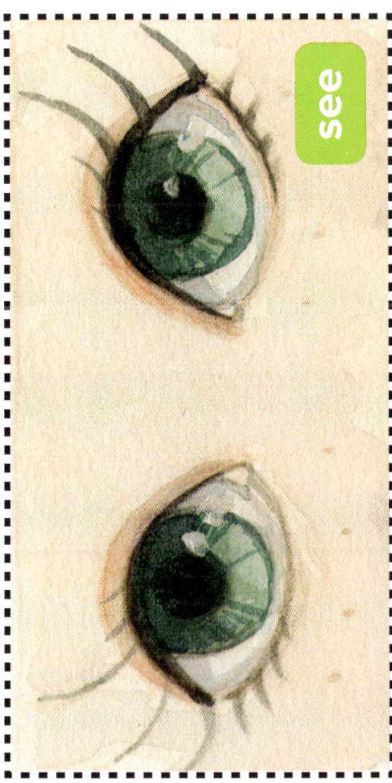

Topic 8 "Let's Explore!"

Topic 9 "Clean Your Room!"

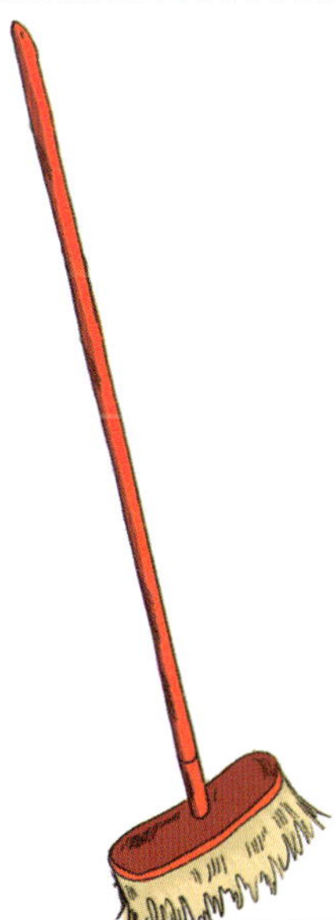

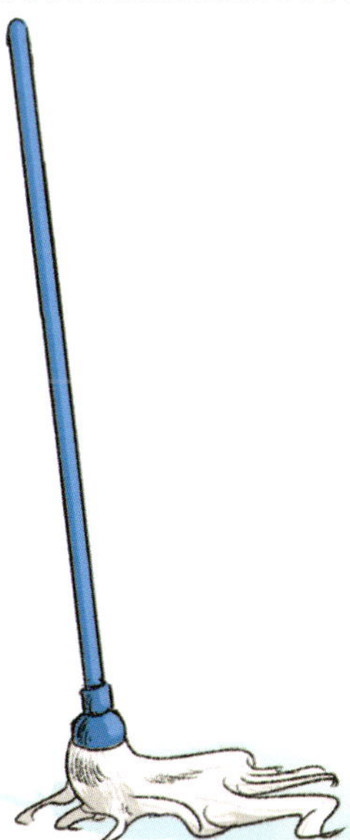

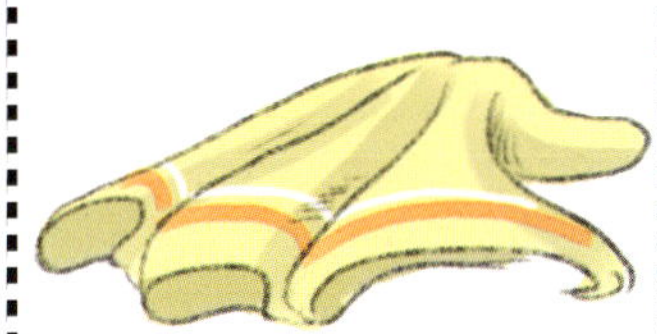